DID YOU KNOW?
WONDERS OF THE WORLD

20 THINGS YOU DIDN'T KNOW ABOUT

STONEHENGE

ELEANOR BRADSHAW

PowerKiDS press

Published in 2025 by The Rosen Publishing Group, Inc.
2544 Clinton Street, Buffalo, NY 14224

Portions of this work were originally authored by Michael Sabatino and published as *20 Fun Facts About Stonehenge*. All new material in this edition was authored by Eleanor Bradshaw.

Editor: Rachael Morlock
Book Design: Tanya Dellaccio Keeney

Photo Credits: Cover Roger Nichol/Shutterstock.com; p. 5 Drone Explorer/Shutterstock.com; p. 6 Kevin Standage/Shutterstock.com; pp. 7, 29 Donna Gibbs-Williams/Shutterstock.com; p. 8 https://upload.wikimedia.org/wikipedia/commons/6/6a/Top_or_Topic_%28CC%2C_Maastricht%29%2C_prehistorische_hakbijl_van_hertshoorn_uit_vuursteenmijn_Rijckholt.jpg; p. 9 https://upload.wikimedia.org/wikipedia/commons/3/37/Stonehenge_004.jpg; p. 10 Keitma/Shutterstock.com; p. 11 M. Vinuesa/Shutterstock.com; p. 12 meunierd/Shutterstock.com; p. 13 Phil Harland/Shutterstock.com; p. 14 https://upload.wikimedia.org/wikipedia/commons/6/6b/The_Stockton_Stone_-_Glacial_Erratic_-_geograph.org.uk_-_1955643.jpg; p. 15 tornadoflight; p. 16 https://upload.wikimedia.org/wikipedia/commons/a/ae/Large_Hammerstone_at_the_Stonehenge_Museum.jpg; p. 17 (main) Paolo Trovo/Shutterstock.com; p. 17 (inset) https://upload.wikimedia.org/wikipedia/commons/d/de/Stonehenge_diagram.png; p. 20 monmii/Shutterstock.com; p. 21 Athip_Taechapongsathon/Shutterstock.com; p. 22 https://upload.wikimedia.org/wikipedia/commons/a/a4/BLEgerton3028Fol30rStonehengeCropped.jpg; p. 23 Nicholas Grey/Shutterstock.com; p. 24 https://upload.wikimedia.org/wikipedia/commons/0/09/Stonehenge_megalith_with_ancient_carvings_April_2005.jpg; p. 25 https://upload.wikimedia.org/wikipedia/commons/a/ab/Stonehenge_Cremation.jpg; p. 26 John Kotlowski/Shutterstock.com; p. 27 Kiev.Victor/Shutterstock.com.

Library of Congress Cataloging-in-Publication Data
Names: Bradshaw, Eleanor, author.
Title: 20 things you didn't know about Stonehenge / Eleanor Bradshaw.
Other titles: Twenty things you did not know about Stonehenge
Description: Buffalo : PowerKids Press, [2025] | Series: Did you know? Wonders of the world | Includes bibliographical references and index.
Identifiers: LCCN 2023057389 (print) | LCCN 2023057390 (ebook) | ISBN 9781499445350 (library binding) | ISBN 9781499445343 (paperback) | ISBN 9781499445367 (ebook)
Subjects: LCSH: Stonehenge (England)–Juvenile literature.
Classification: LCC DA142 .B68 2025 (print) | LCC DA142 (ebook) | DDC 936.2/31–dc23/eng/20240110
LC record available at https://lccn.loc.gov/2023057389
LC ebook record available at https://lccn.loc.gov/2023057390

Manufactured in the United States of America

CPSIA Compliance Information: Batch #CSPK25. For Further Information contact Rosen Publishing at 1-800-237-9932.

CONTENTS

A LOOK AT THE PAST

It's easy to recognize the monument called Stonehenge. The circle of giant stones is located on Salisbury Plain in Wiltshire, England, but it appears in art and stories from around the world.

Stonehenge is a prehistoric monument, which means it comes from a time in the past before written records. Looking at Stonehenge gives us a chance to see the world in the way prehistoric people saw it. We don't know exactly why or how it was created, but the amount of time and effort that went into building Stonehenge tells us that it was of great importance.

Stonehenge was built over about 1,500 years. It took several different shapes over that time. Since its completion, some stones have fallen or been taken from the monument.

THE PEOPLE OF STONEHENGE

DID YOU KNOW?

We don't know who built Stonehenge.

The people who built Stonehenge didn't have written records, but they did leave behind objects. Simple tools made of stone were found underground near Stonehenge. The **structures** that they built also left marks in the earth. **Archaeologists** study these clues to learn about prehistoric people.

These archaeologists are excavating, or digging up, another prehistoric monument in Wiltshire, not far from Stonehenge.

DID YOU KNOW?

People lived near the Stonehenge **site** long before the monument was built.

An area called Amesbury, which includes Stonehenge, lies in the valley of the River Avon. Amesbury is thought to be the oldest settlement in England. People have lived there since 8820 BCE. The first-known structures near Stonehenge were made with large wooden posts between 8500 and 7000 BCE.

EARTH AND STONE

DID YOU KNOW?

The circular henge is about 328 feet (100 m) wide.

A henge is an ancient structure built on flat land and shaped like a circle or an oval. It is surrounded by ditches and a raised ring of earth called a bank. At Stonehenge, people used tools made from animal antlers to dig the circular ditch.

Archaeologists have found picks made from antlers at Stonehenge and other prehistoric sites.

This drawing shows Stonehenge as it would have appeared with all the stones in place around 2200 BCE.

DID YOU KNOW?

Builders brought and arranged the stones in stages.

Builders formed the henge area around 3000 BCE. They also dug 56 holes in which stones could stand in a large circle. These are called Aubrey holes. The largest stones were brought to the site around 2500 BCE. Builders rearranged the stones for the last time around 2200 BCE.

ANCIENT MONUMENTS

DID YOU KNOW?

Stone monuments like Stonehenge are found all over the world.

A dolmen is another type of stone monument. More than 440 prehistoric dolmens were built at the Gochang Dolmen Site in South Korea.

Stonehenge is made of megaliths—very large stones used as monuments or building materials. Stone monuments both big and small can be found in countries all over the world. The word "megalith" comes from the ancient Greek language. *Mega* means "big," and *lithos* means "stone."

The Ring of Brogdar in the Orkney Islands of Scotland was constructed around the same time as Stonehenge. It was made up of 60 standing stones set in a circle.

DID YOU KNOW?

About 1,300 stone circles remain in Britain and Ireland.

Stonehenge is smaller than the nearby stone circle of Avebury. In fact, Avebury is one of the largest in the world! However, the way Stonehenge was built is more advanced. One unusual feature is the post-and-lintel structure in which one stone, the lintel, is placed on top of two vertical stones, the posts.

STONES

DID YOU KNOW?

Stonehenge was built with two main kinds of stone.

The larger stones are called sarsen stones. Many weigh as much as 50,000 pounds (22,680 kg)! The sarsen stones came from about 20 miles (32 km) away. The smaller stones are called bluestones. They weigh about 10,000 pounds (4,536 kg) at the most.

The Heel Stone was probably put up at Stonehenge in the first stage of building. It stands outside the central circle and was not shaped by tools.

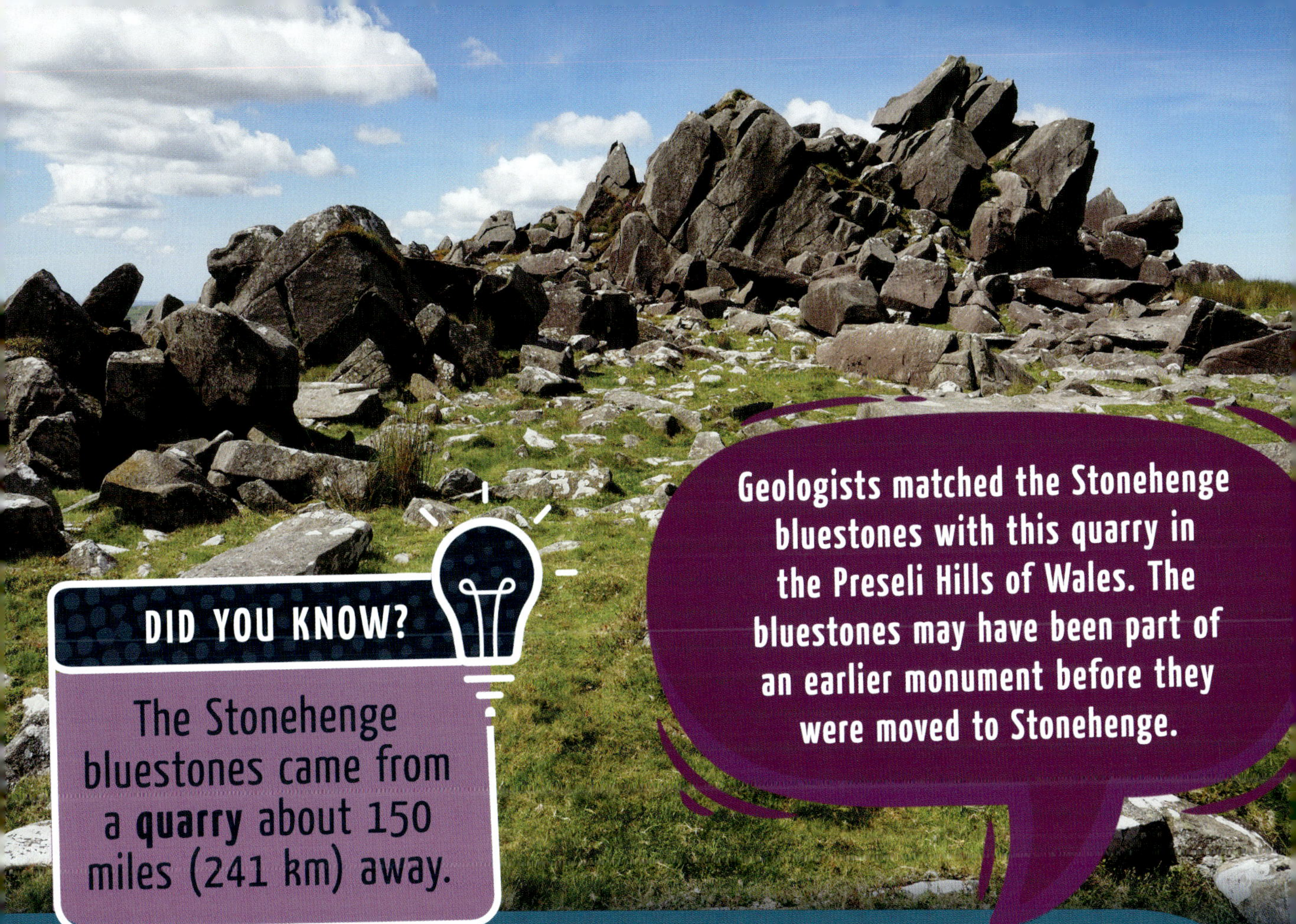

Geologists matched the Stonehenge bluestones with this quarry in the Preseli Hills of Wales. The bluestones may have been part of an earlier monument before they were moved to Stonehenge.

DID YOU KNOW?

The Stonehenge bluestones came from a **quarry** about 150 miles (241 km) away.

Geologists have found the original **source** of Stonehenge's bluestones at a quarry in Wales. Most stone circles are made from local rocks. The faraway source of the bluestones makes Stonehenge unusual. But how did people move the stones so far? Did they travel by land or sea? These questions remain unanswered.

MOVING STONES

DID YOU KNOW?

Glaciers may have moved the stones closer to Stonehenge.

Some geologists argue that glaciers rather than people carried the bluestones from the quarry. They believe a glacier moving slowly over the land may have picked up stones. When the glacier melted, it could have dropped the stones near Salisbury Plain.

The Stockton Stone in Norfolk, England, is an example of a stone that was moved by glaciers and then used as a stone monument.

Some archaeologists think the stones were tied to wooden cages and rolled over logs. A display at the Stonehenge Visitor Centre shows how this would work.

DID YOU KNOW?

The builders of Stonehenge moved huge stones without wheels.

It's possible that enormous stones were set on top of smaller stones and rolled over land. Some people believe the stones were pulled on wooden sleds or floated on **rafts**. Archaeologists have experimented with different ways of moving the giant stones, but the true method is still a mystery.

SHAPING STONES

DID YOU KNOW?

The Stonehenge builders didn't have metal tools.

Builders shaped and moved stones using tools made of stone, wood, and animal parts. They used large hammerstones to break off big pieces of rock. Smaller hammerstones could smooth the stones' surfaces. Builders dug holes in the ground with antler picks. They set the finished stones in the holes using ropes and logs.

This is an example of a large hammerstone.

The stones of Stonehenge's outer ring fit together perfectly thanks to careful shaping. The ring was originally made of 30 sarsen stones.

DID YOU KNOW?

Builders used special joins to make post-and-lintel structures secure.

Bumps on the post stones fit into hollows on the lintel stones. The stones in Stonehenge's outer ring are joined in this manner. Slots connect the ends of these lintels to each other as well. At one point, the curved, joined lintels of the outer ring formed a complete circle.

TIMES OF CHANGE

People have been changing Stonehenge and the area around it for thousands of years. Here are some key dates and events in the history of the monument.

8500–7000 BCE

People raise a few large pine posts nearly 3 feet (0.9 m) wide near the current site. They may have been similar to totem poles.

3000–2935 BCE

Workers dig a circular ditch at the current site to form part of a henge. They dig the Aubrey holes in a ring inside the bank. Human remains are buried in and around the holes.

2640–2480 BCE

People bring sarsen stones to the site and shape them into a circle. Inside the circle, giant post-and-lintel structures called trilithons form a horseshoe shape. Two rows of smaller bluestones are arranged within the circle.

2470–2280 BCE

Workers create an avenue that runs for two miles (3 km) from the monument to the River Avon.

2280–2030 BCE

People move the bluestones to form a circle and an oval inside the sarsen stone ring.

2030–1750 BCE

Workers dig a ring of holes around the outside of the stone circle.

1640–1520 BCE

Workers dig more holes outside the circle. This is the last-known change that builders made to Stonehenge.

STAR CONNECTION

DID YOU KNOW?

People have some wild ideas to explain how Stonehenge was built.

Some say it would have been too hard for ancient people to build Stonehenge without help. One idea claims aliens, or beings from other worlds, visited Earth. Believers say these aliens could have shared their knowledge and taught ancient humans how to build such an outstanding monument.

Although alien aid can't be ruled out, it's more likely that humans in prehistoric times were just as smart and creative as humans today!

People may have gathered at Stonehenge at special times of the year to view the stars or watch the sun rise and set.

DID YOU KNOW?

The people who created Stonehenge understood **astronomy**.

While no one's sure what Stonehenge was used for, it does seem to be connected to the sun. The monument was built to line up with the path of the sun on the longest and shortest days of the year. Some people think Stonehenge was used as a calendar to mark holidays and track changes in the seasons.

MAGICAL TALES

DID YOU KNOW?

Some tales connect the **wizard** Merlin with Stonehenge.

In **legends** from the past, Merlin served King Arthur. One popular tale says an army of 15,000 men tried but failed to move stones to build Stonehenge. They asked Merlin for help. Merlin used his magical powers to move the stones to Salisbury Plain and put the monument together.

A drawing from between 1325 and 1350 CE shows Merlin at Stonehenge. In this story, Merlin calls on giants from Ireland to build the monument.

Why did builders bring the bluestones to Stonehenge from so far away? Perhaps they believed these stones had special, healing properties.

DID YOU KNOW?

Many tales claim that the stones have magical powers.

Some people may have traveled to Stonehenge seeking magical or medical help. It's possible they believed Stonehenge had the power to heal. Studies of the human remains buried around Stonehenge show that people traveled long distances to arrive at the site.

HUMAN TRACES

DID YOU KNOW?

People left their mark on Stonehenge long after it was built.

Using a special laser, archaeologists have uncovered many secrets of Stonehenge's past—including **graffiti**. These markings range from a few hundred years old to thousands of years old. People of the Bronze Age carved dagger and ax shapes into the monument more than 3,000 years ago.

Can you find the ax and dagger carved into this stone?

Bodies were burned before being buried in the Aubrey holes. Archaeologists have found pieces of bone left behind. Between 150 and 240 people were buried in this way at Stonehenge.

DID YOU KNOW?

People may have traveled great distances to honor and bury their dead at Stonehenge.

Even before the monument was built, people were buried near Stonehenge in mounds of earth called long barrows. Starting around 3000 BCE, human remains were buried in and near the Aubrey holes. Later, Bronze Age people buried their dead in hundreds of round barrows nearby.

STONEHENGE TODAY

DID YOU KNOW?

Stonehenge is more popular than ever.

The ancient site gets over 1 million visitors a year. That wasn't always the case. Only about 20,000 people visited Stonehenge in 1920. Today, the summer **solstice** alone draws a crowd of thousands. Modern visitors are only allowed inside the stone circle during the solstice.

The summer solstice is the longest day of the year. This is a popular day for visitors to gather at Stonehenge.

Some of the stones at Stonehenge have been damaged by time and weather or removed by earlier generations. UNESCO's goal is to keep the rest of Stonehenge standing for as long as possible!

DID YOU KNOW?

Stonehenge is a protected site.

UNESCO is an agency, or group, that recognizes and protects historic locations around the world. The group named Stonehenge a World Heritage Site in 1986. This means that Stonehenge will be protected and kept in good shape for many years to come. The landmarks around Stonehenge are also protected for future **generations** to visit and study.

THE PAST

A sense of magic and mystery will always surround Stonehenge, but there's a lot we do know about the monument. Thanks to new ways of studying the past, we can piece together facts and imagine what life must have been like for prehistoric people.

It took 100 generations of builders to dig the pits and ditches, move the stones, and build the monument. Over those generations, daily life changed, and so did values and beliefs. But 5,000 years later, Stonehenge still stands.

Stonehenge continues to be a meeting place where people can look back and honor their **ancestors**.

GLOSSARY

ancestor: One of the people from whom a person is descended.

archaeologist: Someone who studies the tools and other objects left behind by ancient people.

astronomy: The science of stars, planets, and other bodies in space.

generation: A group of people born and living during the same time.

geologist: A scientist who studies the history of Earth as shown through its rocks, soil, and landforms.

graffiti: Pictures or words painted or drawn on a wall or structure.

legend: A story coming down from the past that is popularly accepted but can't be checked.

quarry: A place where people dig for stone for building.

raft: A flat structure used for floating on water.

site: The place where something is located.

solstice: The time of year when the sun is farthest north (summer solstice) or farthest south (winter solstice) of the equator.

source: A person, place, or thing from which something comes or where it can be found.

structure: A building or another object that is constructed.

wizard: A person who has magical powers.

FOR MORE INFORMATION

BOOKS

Gaertner, Meg. *Stonehenge.* Mendota Heights, MN: Apex, 2022.

Howell, Izzi. *The Genius of the Stone, Bronze, and Iron Ages.* St. Catherines, ON: Crabtree Publishing Company, 2020.

WEBSITES

English Heritage
www.stonehengeskyscape.co.uk/
Take a virtual tour of Stonehenge and view the position of the sun and stars on this site from English Heritage.

National Geographic Kids
www.natgeokids.com/uk/discover/history/general-history/stonehenge-facts/
Find facts, photos of Stonehenge, and information about the latest discoveries on this page.

Publisher's note to educators and parents: Our editors have carefully reviewed these websites to ensure that they are suitable for students. Many websites change frequently, however, and we cannot guarantee that a site's future contents will continue to meet our high standards of quality and educational value. Be advised that students should be closely supervised whenever they access the internet.

INDEX